Food and Festivals

A Flavour of GERMANY

Other titles:

Cover photograph: A German delicatessen counter showing many different types of meat.

Title page: Traditional German meats and cheeses.

Contents page: Musicians, dressed up for the festival of *Carneval,* in Cologne.

All Wayland books encourage children to read and help them improve their literacy.

✓ The contents page, page numbers, headings and index help locate specific pieces of information.

✓ The glossary reinforces alphabetic knowledge and extends vocabulary.

✓ The further information section suggests other books dealing with the same subject.

✓ Find out more about how this book is specifically relevant to the National Literacy Strategy on page 31.

First published in 1999 by Wayland Publishers Limited, 61 Western Road, Hove, East Sussex, BN3 1JD, England

© Copyright 1999 Wayland Publishers Limited

Series editor: Polly Goodman
Book editor: Margot Richardson
Designer: Tim Mayer

British Library Cataloguing in Publication Data
Hirst, Mike
  A Flavour of Germany. – (Food and Festivals)
  1. Cookery, German – Juvenile literature
  2. Festivals – Germany – Juvenile literature
  3. Food habits – Germany – Juvenile literature
  4. Social life and customs – 20th century – Juvenile literature
  I. Title
  641.5'943

ISBN 0 7502 2560 2

Typeset by Mayer Media
Printed and bound by EuroGrafica, Vicenza, Italy

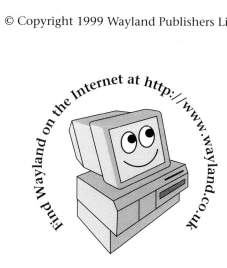

Find Wayland on the Internet at http://www.wayland.co.uk

CONTENTS

Germany and its Food

DENMARK

NORTH
SEA

BALTIC
SEA

N

NETHERLANDS

POLAND

Hamburg

Weser

Elbe

Berlin

BELGIUM LUX

GERMANY

Cologne

Rhine

Frankfurt am Main

CZECH
REPUBLIC

FRANCE

Nuremberg

GERMANY

Germany's place in the world

BAVARIA

Danube

Munich

AUSTRIA

SWITZERLAND

Zugspitze

| 0 | 100 | 200 km |

| 0 | 100 miles |

WHEAT AND RYE

Wheat and rye are both grain crops. They are made into flour which is used to make German bread. Most Germans eat bread twice a day, or more.

DAIRY PRODUCTS

Milk, butter, cheeses and yoghurts are all popular dairy products in Germany. People eat cheese for breakfast and at tea time.

FISH

Fish are caught in the sea off the north coast of Germany. Some fish also come from rivers and lakes. Rollmops and Bismarck herrings are popular German fish dishes.

GRAPES

Grapes are grown in vineyards, often on the sides of valleys to catch the sun. Many of Germany's grapes are made into wines. German wines are famous all over the world.

MEAT

Many German recipes include meat. Sausages are usually made from pork. There are special rules that say exactly how sausages should be made.

VEGETABLES

Germans eat many different types of vegetables. Potatoes and cabbage, which grow well in a cool climate, are most often found in traditional cooking.

Food and Farming

▼ In the countryside, some families have worked on the same small farm for two or three hundred years.

With over 80 million people, Germany is one of the biggest countries in Europe. It has busy towns and cities, and large areas of beautiful countryside. Between the flat coast in the north and the high mountains of the south there are rolling hills, farmland and thick forests.

Traditional food

▲ An *Imbissstube* is a snack bar that sells traditional food such as sausages.

Germany is a modern, wealthy country, but people still enjoy eating traditional dishes handed down from the past. Wherever you go, from a tiny village to the large capital city of Berlin, you will find someone sitting down to a meal of traditional German food. It might be frankfurter sausages, pumpernickel (a heavy brown bread) or pickled cabbage called sauerkraut (pronounced 'sour-crout').

FIRST-DAY TREAT

On their first day at school, German children have a special treat: a huge cardboard cone, filled with sweets and chocolates.

BROTPREISE
Doppelbrot 1.20
5er Brezen 3.50
10er Brezen 5.50
Zwiebelbrot 3,—
Vintschgauer 3 —
Wachauerweckerl
Käsestangen 2,50

▲ Pretzels are made from salty bread twisted into a ring shape.

Bread and cakes

If you go into a German bakery, the first thing you notice is the huge choice of different breads. There are over 1,200 kinds of bread roll, each one made in a slightly different way. As well as bread, many bakeries also sell a big choice of cakes.

ORGANIC FARMING

Organic farmers do not use artificial fertilizers or pesticides on their crops. They feed farm animals natural foods without any extra chemicals. People who eat organic food believe it is healthier and tastes better. Organic food is very popular in Germany.

Most Germans eat some brown bread every day. The flour for this bread is made from grains of wheat or rye, and the mixture includes yeast to make the dough puff up in the oven. Germans also like a heavier type of brown bread which uses a mixture of sugar and water instead of yeast. This dark brown bread is useful because it stays fresh for a long time: up to three or four weeks.

This photograph ▶ shows a typical evening meal of bread, cold meats, cheese, sauerkraut and pickled gherkins. Many Germans eat their main, hot meal at midday.

Regional food

Every region of Germany, and every big city, has its own special recipes. A *Berliner* is a kind of doughnut, named after the capital city. A frankfurter is a sausage, originally from Frankfurt am Main.

In the seaside towns and cities in the north of the country, fish caught by local boats are widely eaten. Common recipes use herrings, sprats and mackerel.

Black Forest gâteau is a delicious cake from the Black Forest in the south-west. In summer, this region has warm, sunny weather which is good for growing many kinds of fruit.

DOUGHNUT TROUBLE

In 1963, the American President John F. Kennedy visited Berlin. He wanted to give his support to the city, so he said '*Ich bin ein Berliner*'. He thought this meant 'I am a Berliner', but unfortunately, in German, it means 'I am a doughnut'.

▼ Black Forest gâteau is flavoured with cherries and chocolate.

Food from other lands

Today, many German towns have communities of Turkish or Greek people, who have come to live and work there with their families. They have introduced their own food to Germany. Nowadays, Germans are likely to eat Turkish kebabs and Greek pitta bread as well as sausages and sauerkraut.

▲ Shops and restaurants selling Turkish and Greek food are found in many parts of Germany. This take-away shop is selling Turkish pizza.

WHAT ARE BISMARCK HERRINGS?

Bismarck herrings are a type of fish pickled in vinegar. They are named after a famous German chancellor, or prime minister, Otto von Bismarck, who lived from 1815 to 1898. Bismarck's doctor told him that eating the small fish was good for his health, so the chancellor's cook invented a way of keeping them fresh by putting them in vinegar.

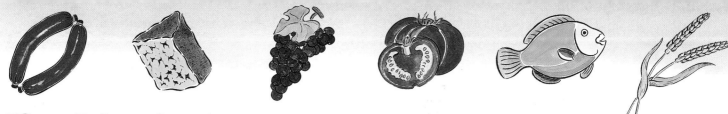

Religions and Festivals

The largest religion in Germany is Christianity. There are two main groups of Christians: Catholics and Protestants. Christmas and Easter are the main Christian festivals, which all Christian Germans celebrate. Other festivals are more important for just one religious group or region in Germany.

▼ These villagers from Bavaria are wearing traditional costumes for a religious festival.

Catholic churches have special services and processions for the holiday of Corpus Christi in June. In November, Protestants have a quiet day of prayer and remembrance, called *Buss-und Bettag* (pronounced 'Booss-oond Bay-tag'). *'Buss'* means 'repentance' and *'bettag'* means 'quiet thinking'.

Many of Germany's Turkish people are Muslims. They celebrate the festivals of Islam, such as Id-ul-Fitr.

Easter

On Easter Sunday, German children hunt around their homes and gardens for Easter eggs. They look for eggs that the Easter hare has brought for them during the night.

▲ Germans like to paint their own Easter eggs. These ones have traditional patterns painted on them.

Day of Unity

In 1949, four years after the end of the Second World War, Germany was divided into two separate countries, East Germany and West Germany. It was very difficult to travel between the two countries, and families and friends were split up. On 3 October 1990, the two countries were finally brought back together again. Since then, 3 October has been a holiday for everyone in Germany. It is called 'The Day of German Unity'.

▼ This dish is called 'strength bread'. It comes from Hamburg, but people eat it all over Germany today. There is a recipe for this dish on the opposite page.

Hamburg 'Strength Bread'

EQUIPMENT

Knife
Frying pan
Egg slice

INGREDIENTS

1 slice of rye bread
Butter or margarine
1 of slice ham

1 egg
A little oil for frying
Salt

Spread a little butter or margarine on the slice of bread.

Put the slice of ham on to the buttered bread.

Ask an adult to heat the oil in the frying pan. Then break the egg into the pan and sprinkle on a pinch of salt.

When the egg is cooked, carefully take it out of the pan, and put it on top of the ham.

Always be careful with frying. Ask an adult to help you.

Carneval

Carneval takes place every February, just before the beginning of Lent. For Christians, Lent is a time for quiet thinking and fasting. Some people give up eating a favourite food during Lent, such as sweets or chocolate.

Before the fasting period of Lent begins, everyone enjoys the parties and parades of *Carneval*.

Marching bands are ▶ an important part of the *Carneval* parades.

16

Carneval begins

The biggest celebration of *Carneval* takes place in the city of Cologne. The festival starts on a Thursday, when the mayor of Cologne hands over the keys of his city to a 'Carnival Prince'. The next few days are 'crazy days', when people have parties and parades. They go out into the streets wearing face paints and fancy-dress costumes. If you walk around the city, you meet clowns, milkmaids and old-fashioned soldiers!

▼ A band, dressed in rag costumes, play in front of Cologne cathedral.

Rose Monday Parade

The biggest *Carneval* parade is held on 'Rose Monday'. Over 7,000 people march through the city with horses, floats and musicians. People in the parade throw more than 40 tonnes of sweets and 100,000 chocolates into the crowds. The paraders even throw flowers and little containers of Eau-de-Cologne, a kind of perfume made in the city.

The words of a popular *Carneval* folk song say 'By Ash Wednesday, it's all over.' After such a huge party, everyone is ready for the start of Lent.

▲ Potato cakes are a speciality from Cologne. They are popular all year round, not just at *Carneval.* There is a recipe for this dish on page 19.

FISH DISHES

One Christian tradition is to stop eating meat during the 40 days of Lent. In Cologne, on Ash Wednesday (the first day of Lent) many restaurants have special fish menus.

Potato Cakes

EQUIPMENT

Potato peeler   Mixing bowl
Grater   Mixing spoon
Sieve   Frying pan
Chopping knife

INGREDIENTS

1 kg potatoes (new potatoes are best)
1 onion
2 eggs
Pinch of salt
125 g plain flour
Pinch of nutmeg
Cooking oil

Peel the potatoes and grate into a sieve, using a rough grater. Leave the potato in the sieve to drain.

Chop the onion finely. Beat the eggs in the bowl. Mix in the onion, grated potatoes, flour, salt and nutmeg.

Ask an adult to heat the oil gently in a frying pan. Put spoonfuls of the mixture into the pan, and flatten into mini-pancake shapes.

Fry both sides of the cakes until golden brown. Serve hot. The potato cakes taste really good eaten with some apple sauce.

Always be careful with chopping and frying. Ask an adult to help you.

Autumn Festivals

Autumn is a time for many local festivals. In the countryside, the harvest is over and people celebrate the end of the hard work. Village churches hold special services of thanksgiving.

▼ The *Oktoberfest* in Munich opens with a colourful procession.

Oktoberfest

The biggest and best-known autumn festival is the *Oktoberfest*, or October Festival. This takes place in the city of Munich, and was first held in 1810 to celebrate the wedding of the future king of Bavaria. Today, Bavaria is Germany's largest region, and people in Munich are very proud of their Bavarian traditions.

At *Oktoberfest*, a huge funfair is set up, with hundreds of rides and stalls. From the top of the massive ferris wheel, on a clear day, you can see as far as the *Zugspitze*, (pronounced 'Zoog-shpitser'), Germany's highest mountain, far away to the south.

▲ Crowds of people fill the autumn fairground at Munich's *Oktoberfest.*

Festival food

▲ Inside a food tent at the Oktoberfest.

Food at the Oktoberfest is served in big tents, where people sit at long, wooden tables. They eat pretzels, and sausages are on the menu too. In Munich, the favourites are white sausage, which you eat by sucking the meat out of the sausage skin. Adults might also have a large glass of beer, made in one of Munich's local breweries. As they eat, visitors listen to folk music, played by a band of wind instruments.

FOOD LAWS

Traditional foods are carefully controlled in Germany. Every type of sausage is made to strict rules, and all beer is made following a special law that was set down in 1516, called the 'Purity Law'.

◀ White sausage is always served with mustard.

St. Martin's Day

St. Martin's Day, or Martinmas, on 11 November, is another autumn festival. It celebrates the legend of St. Martin.

The legend tells how Martin was born into a wealthy family and grew up to be a soldier. One day, he met a beggar who was starving and dying of cold. Martin felt so sorry for the beggar that he took off his own cloak and cut it in two. He gave half to the beggar. Soon afterwards, the beggar came back to Martin in a dream and said that he was really Jesus Christ in disguise. Jesus told the angels of Martin's good deed.

▲ In this old painting, St. Martin uses his sword to cut his cloak in two.

Martin decided to become a priest. Soon, he was made a bishop. However, he was so shy that he hid in a farmyard when he heard the news. No one could find him until some geese started cackling and gave his hiding place away. Because of this story, St. Martin's day is connected with one particular kind of food: roast goose. This is still the traditional meal to eat on 11 November in Germany.

Food at Martinmas

In the Middle Ages, November was a very busy time. Farmers never had enough food to keep their animals through the winter, so many animals were killed on St. Martin's Day. The meat was dried and salted to stop it going bad.

Today, on St. Martin's Day, people remember the stories about the saint's good deeds.

▲ Baked apples are a popular autumn food around St. Martin's Day. There is a recipe for this dish on the opposite page.

Baked Apples

EQUIPMENT

Apple corer
Baking tray
Small sieve

INGREDIENTS

Four apples   Cinnamon
Handful of raisins   Nutmeg
A little butter   Icing sugar

Using the apple corer, take the core out of each apple.

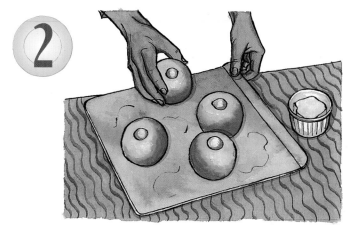

Put the cored apples on to a greased baking tray.

Stuff the hole in each apple with raisins. Sprinkle with a little nutmeg and cinnamon and put a dab of butter on top.

Ask an adult to bake the apples for 20 minutes, at 220 °C/gas mark 6. When they are cooked, sprinkle with icing sugar to serve.

Be careful with the hot baking tray. Ask an adult to help you.

Advent and Christmas

▼ This huge electric advent calendar is in Berlin. It counts down the days to Christmas.

Christmas, which celebrates the birth of Jesus, is the biggest festival of the year in Germany. The four Sundays before Christmas are called Advent. During this time, Germans enjoy getting ready for Christmas Day, on 25 December. Many towns have a special Christmas market where decorations, presents and Christmas foods are sold.

Christmas trees

The tradition of Christmas trees comes from Germany, and most German families have one in their home at Christmas. No one is quite sure how the tradition began. Some people think that the first trees were used as scenery for religious plays, which were put on at Christmas during the Middle Ages.

▲ Children at a Christmas market in Kayserberg.

St. Nicholas

Another European tradition that started in Germany is the one of St. Nicholas giving presents to children. This tradition goes back several centuries. Today, on 6 December, children still receive small presents from St. Nicholas.

▲ This picture shows St. Nicholas throwing apples to children on 6 December.

Christmas Cakes

There are many delicious Christmas recipes. *Stollen* is a type of rich Christmas cake from the city of Dresden. It contains dried fruits and, in the middle, a thick layer of marsipan. *Lebkuchen* (pronounced 'leb-cooken') are a mixture between cakes and biscuits, and are made with spices.

▲ You can eat this little house. It is made out of *Lebkuchen*.

SPICE FAIR

Lebkuchen were invented in the Middle Ages, in the city of Nuremberg. Every year, the city held a fair, where merchants sold spices from far-off countries. These spices (ginger, cloves and cinnamon) give *Lebkuchen* their special taste.

These biscuits are called ▶ *Spritzgebäck* (pronounced 'Shprits-gebeck'), which means 'squirt biscuits'. This is because of the way you squeeze the shapes out of an icing bag when you make them. There is a recipe for these biscuits on the opposite page.

Christmas Biscuits

EQUIPMENT

Mixing bowl
Mixing spoon
Baking tray
Icing bag and large star nozzle

INGREDIENTS

120 g butter
80 g caster sugar
2 eggs
250 g self-raising flour
Few drops of vanilla essence

Let the butter soften. Then mix the butter and sugar with a wooden spoon until the mixture is light. Add the eggs, flour and vanilla essence.

Grease a baking tray. Put the biscuit mixture into the icing bag,

Squeeze small circles on to the tray in biscuit shapes.

Ask an adult to bake the biscuits for 15 minutes at 175 °C/gas mark 4.

Be careful with the hot baking tray. Ask an adult to help you.

Glossary

Bakery A place where bread and cakes are made.

Catholics One of the two main groups in the Christian religion. The leader of the Catholic Church is the Pope, who lives in Rome, Italy.

Fertilizers Substances that make soil more fertile, so that it grows more grass or crops.

Floats A platform on wheels, used in a parade.

Gateau Cake, usually made with cream and a rich topping.

Id-ul-Fitr A Muslim festival, held at the end of Ramadan, a month of fasting.

Kebab Pieces of meat, cooked on a grill or barbecue.

Lent Period of 40 weekdays just before Easter. During this period, Christians remember the time when Jesus Christ went into the wilderness.

Pesticides Chemicals that kill pests which eat crops, usually insects.

Pickled Food put in salty water or vinegar, to stop it from going bad.

Pitta bread A type of flat bread that comes from Greece.

Protestants One of the two main groups in the Christian religion. The first German Protestants had a leader called Martin Luther, who left the Catholic Church in 1517.

Second World War A war between 1939 and 1945, when many countries in the world fought against Germany, Italy and Japan.

Traditional Something based on customs or beliefs that have lasted for many years. Traditions are part of the history of a country.

Picture acknowledgements

AKG photo 27 bottom; Bipinchandra 26, 28 top; Anthony Blake Photo Library *title page*, 13/Maximilian; Cephas 5 mid right/Nigel Blythe, 6/David Burnett, 9, 10, 16/Nigel Blythe, 22; Chapel Studios/Zul Mukhida 14, 18, 24, 28 bottom; Impact 7/Michael Mirecki; e.t. archive 23; Robert Harding Picture Library 5 mid-left, 5 bottom right/Adam Woolfitt, 8; Pictor Uniphoto 22; S.O.A. Photo Agency/Peter Thomann 27 top; The Stockmarket Photo Agency Inc *cover* and 5 bottom left, 12; Tony Stone Images 20/Stephen Studd, 21/Joerg Hardtke; Trip Photo Library/B. Anthony, *contents page* and 17; Wayland Picture Library 5 top left, 5 top right, 11.
Fruit and vegetable artwork by Tina Barber.
Step-by-step recipe artwork by Judy Stevens.

Topic Web and Resources

MATHS

Using and understanding measure of weight (recipes).

Using and understanding simple fractions.

Using and reading weighing scales.

SCIENCE

Food and nutrition.

Changing materials by sieving, dissolving and heating.

GEOGRAPHY

Locality study: Germany.

Weather in a European country.

Farming.

Comparing physical landscapes.

Influence of human activity on landscapes and vice versa: the kinds of food grown and eaten in Germany.

How land is used.

Geographical knowledge of main cities and features of Western Europe.

MODERN FOREIGN LANGUAGES

German words connected with food.

People, places and customs.

Everyday activities: food.

Food & Festivals TOPIC WEB

HISTORY

History of post-war Germany.

Life in the Middle Ages.

ENGLISH

Investigating traditional stories and legends associated with festivals which are still celebrated today.

Reading and understanding instructional text (recipes).

Practise non-fiction writing by making menus of German food.

DESIGN AND TECHNOLOGY

Designing typically German meals.

Designing and making packaging for German food.

Using kitchen equipment to make German food.

RE

Christian festivals, including Lent, Easter, Harvest, Advent and Christmas.

Legends of saints: St. Martin.

BOOKS TO READ

Country Topics: Germany by Rachel Wright and Neil Morris (Franklin Watts, 1993)

Festivals: Christmas by Clare Chandler (Wayland, 1996)

Festivals: Easter by Philip Sauvain (Wayland, 1997)

Fiesta! Germany by Tessa Paul (Franklin Watts, 1997)

Land and Peoples of Germany by Ed Needham (Franklin Watts, 1996)

We Come From Germany by Mike Hirst (Wayland, 1999)

This book meets the following specific objectives of the National Literacy Strategy's Framework for Teaching:

✓ Range of work in non-fiction: instructional text including simple recipes, labels, captions, lists, glossary and index.

✓ Vocabulary extension: words linked to particular topics (food words) and technical words from work in other subjects (geography and food science).

Index

Page numbers in **bold** mean there is a photograph on the page.